HABITATS

WETLANDS

EWAN M^cLEISH

Thomson Learning
New York

HABITATS

Coasts	Mountains
Deserts	Polar Regions
Forests	Rivers and Lakes
Grasslands	Seas and Oceans
Islands	Wetlands

Cover: Marshes on Laeso Island, Denmark
Title page: The Okefenokee swamps in Georgia
Contents page: Wildflowers blooming in an English water meadow

First published in the United States in 1996 by
Thomson Learning
New York, NY

Published in Great Britain in 1995 by Wayland (Publishers) Ltd.

U.S. copyright © 1996 Thomson Learning

U.K. copyright © 1995 Wayland (Publishers) Ltd.

Library of Congress Cataloging-in-Publication Data
McLeish, Ewan.
Wetlands / Ewan McLeish.
     p.   cm.—(Habitats)
   Summary: A geography book on the world's wetlands showing
how they are formed, why they are important, and what can be done
to safeguard them for the future.
   Includes bibliographical references and index.
   ISBN 1-56847-319-2 (hc)
   1. Wetlands—Juvenile literature. 2. Wetland ecology—Juvenile
literature. [1. Wetlands. 2. Wetland ecology. 3. Ecology.] I. Title.
II. Series.
GB622.M36   1996
574.5'26325—dc20   95-34465

Printed in Italy

CONTENTS

1. WHERE THE WATER MEETS THE LAND

At such a time I found out that the dark flat wilderness beyond the churchyard, intersected with dykes and mounds and gates, with scattered cattle feeding on it, was the marshes; and that the distant savage lair from which the wind was rushing, was the sea.

Charles Dickens, *Great Expectations*

Marshes like the one Charles Dickens describes above can seem frightening. They are often thought of as lonely and desolate and even dangerous. Marshes can be all of these things, but they are also important habitats for many animals and plants and are frequently dramatic and beautiful places.

Marshes are just one of the many different types of habitat known as wetlands. Wetlands have played an important role in the lives of humans for

A map showing the main areas in the world where wetlands can be found

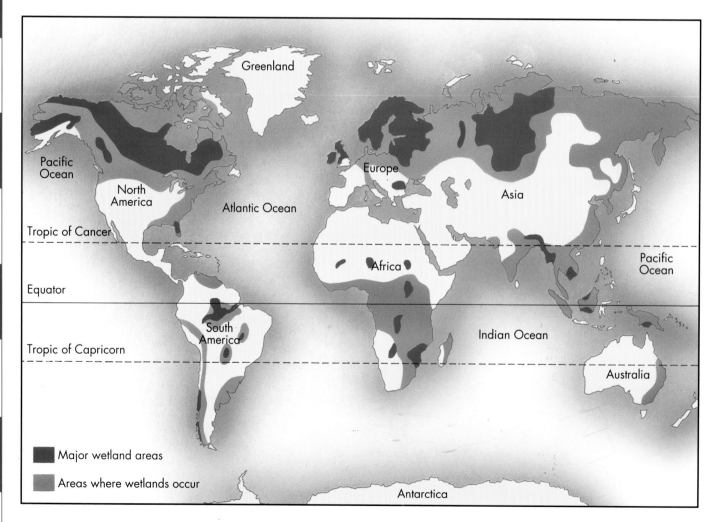

Major wetland areas

Areas where wetlands occur

thousands of years, providing food, fuel, and shelter. But people have not always treated these fragile places with respect. Now many wetland areas are threatened, and some have already been destroyed. This book shows how wetlands are formed, why they are important, and what can be done to safeguard them for the future.

Where are wetlands?

Wetlands are found wherever there is plenty of rainfall or where water does not evaporate or drain away as soon as it enters the soil. Often the soil surface is covered with water, either permanently or at some time during the year.

Above A cypress swamp in South Carolina. The trees are growing in water.

Right Palms and bulrushes growing in a nature reserve in Fakahatchee, Florida.

5

Wetlands can be found all over the world; they are not limited to particular climatic areas as hot, dry deserts or tropical forests are. Wetlands can even occur on sloping ground or on hilltops if the conditions are suitable.

The wild bogs or marshes in the low-lying parts of northern Europe and North America are wetlands. So are different kinds of seashore, such as areas near estuaries where large expanses of mudflats or salt marsh are exposed to both salt water from the sea and fresh water from rivers.

Huge areas of wetland can be found in the land drained by giant rivers, such as the Amazon in South America and the Mississippi in the United States. Swamps describe wetlands that are dominated by trees, such as the tropical swamps of the Florida Everglades. In Botswana, Central Africa, the Okavango Delta creates some 7,000 square miles of wetland wilderness amid the sands of the Kalahari desert.

Above An Aborigine boy fishing in a tropical swamp in Australia's Northern Territory. Wetlands provide a rich source of food for the local people.

Occurring in sheltered, muddy estuaries in tropical and subtropical areas in parts of southern India, Southeast Asia, and northern Australia are mangrove swamps, named after the salt-resistant trees that grow there. Far to the north, beyond the Arctic Circle, lie the tundra peatlands, vast wet areas of moss, and stunted trees that stretch to the horizon.

Right A tundra wetland. The ponds have been made by beavers building dams across the streams.

Left A young boy in his boat, made entirely from reeds, on a lake in Peru in South America

Habitats for all

All wetlands are important habitats for wildlife. For example, marshes are rich in nutrients and support a great variety of plants and animals—especially birds. Reeds grow there, and the reed beds provide an ideal home for the rare, solitary bittern, a wading bird that hunts fish, frogs, and small snakes among the reed bases. Small, insect-eating birds nest among the tall stems, while a powerful predator, the harrier hawk, feeds on the smaller birds or mammals, such as water voles, who have also made their home there.

The water itself of a wetland area is an ideal breeding ground for many species of insects, such as dragonflies and mosquitoes, which spend part of their lives as aquatic larvae. When they emerge as flying adults, many of them are snapped up by wetland birds and other insect-eating animals.

In the Florida Everglades, living among the water-loving swamp cypress and mangrove trees, are giant alligators, crab-eating raccoons, and many different kinds of fish. In contrast, the Okavango in Africa is home to hippos,

Below Elephants stand watchfully on the edge of the Chobe River in Botswana, while hippos wallow in the water to avoid the heat of the midday sun.

8

crocodiles, spectacular pied kingfishers, and countless thousands of migratory waterbirds. In the dryer areas, antelope, such as water buck and impala, mingle with gemsbok seeking refuge from the surrounding desert.

The relationship between people and wetlands is a delicate one. We have to look at ways of making sure that we protect these valuable habitats, both for ourselves and for the animals and plants that live in them.

Left A bittern in a Polish wetland grabs a fish with its dagger-like bill.

Flying eyes

The dragonfly spends much of its life as an underwater larva, preying on other insects, tadpoles, and even small fish. It catches these with powerful jaws that shoot out from behind a movable "mask." Finally it leaves the water, crawls up a reed stem, and splits its skin to allow the magnificent winged adult to emerge. The dragonfly is still a hunter, taking butterflies and mosquitoes on the wing. Two enormous eyes, making up 80 percent of its head, make it a formidable predator.

A dragonfly rests on a twig of heather.

2. THE CREATION OF MARSHES AND BOGS

Nature is always going through changes. A piece of bare land is soon taken over by quick-growing plants whose seeds were blown there by the wind. These are replaced by slower-growing but longer-lived plants. These, too, gradually make way for larger, more shrubby plants, and finally trees may take over. This process is known as succession.

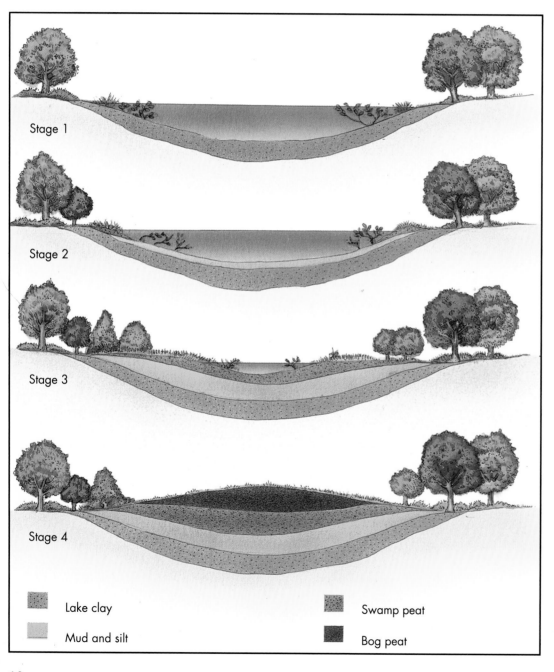

Stage 1

Stage 2

Stage 3

Stage 4

Lake clay

Mud and silt

Swamp peat

Bog peat

Left Formation of a marsh.
Stages 1 and 2: Silt and mud build up, allowing plants to grow across the lake.
Stage 3: Plant material is trapped, building up a layer of peat.
Stage 4: Later in the succession, the marsh may be invaded by bog mosses, which build up domes of peat above the water level (a raised bog).

A typical temperate, lowland marsh in the Netherlands. This marsh provides an excellent habitat for small birds and other animals.

The birth and death of a marsh

Wetlands, too, go through the process of succession. In deep water—a lake, for example—plants grow under the water, fully submerged. Gradually, fine particles of mud or silt, which are carried into the lake by rivers or streams or are washed in from the lakesides, settle on the bottom. Parts of the lake slowly become shallower until it is possible for rooted plants with floating leaves, such as water lilies, to grow.

Later, as the lake becomes shallower still, plants that can grow in water but keep most of their stems above the water level begin to take over. These plants, known as emergent plants, include reeds and bulrushes. The stems of these emergent plants trap still more material flowing into the lake, including humus (dead plant remains).

11

Slowly, the level of silt and humus builds up, forming a thick layer of peat, until the area is flooded only in the winter. The land becomes too dry for the reed swamp plants to survive there, and other plants and moisture-loving trees, such as the alder and willow, begin to invade the dryer ground. More and more plant material builds up, and even the alders and willows may be replaced by trees that are more suited to dryer soil, such as birch or pine.

In this way a marsh or a fen is created, exists for a time—perhaps a thousand years or longer—and then gradually makes way for another type of habitat.

"Murdered" man found in bog

About thirty years ago some peat cutters found the perfectly preserved body of a man six feet below the surface of a Danish bog. They reported their find to the police, thinking a murder had been committed. Scientists concluded, however, that the body was over two thousand years old and was probably a sacrifice to an ancient goddess of fertility. The acid conditions and low oxygen in the bog had prevented the body from decomposing.

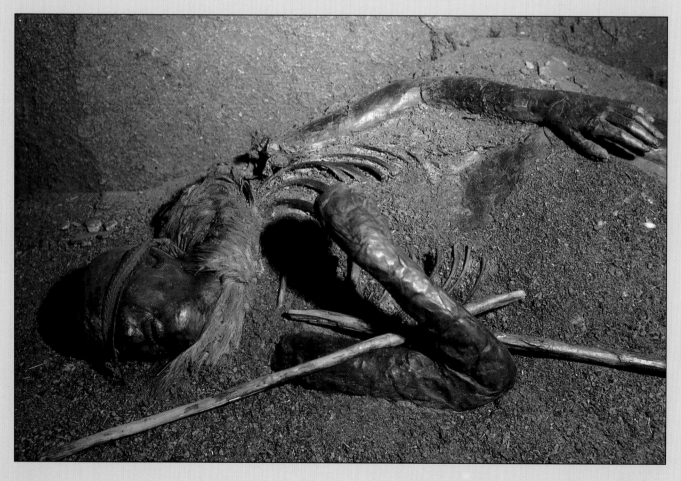

More than one thousand ancient bodies have been found preserved in peat bogs in northern Germany, Scandinavia, and Great Britain. Acids in the bog color the skin, so it looks like leather.

Sphagnum moss, also called peat moss. Sometimes this moss grows over open water and shakes when someone walks on it. Such bogs are called "quaking bogs."

Bogs and bug-eating plants

Wetlands, however, are not always created through the process of succession. On higher ground, where rainfall is heavy and rocks are hard, a different series of events takes place. The permanently wet soil, made slightly acid by the hard rocks beneath, is invaded by an amazing moss called sphagnum. This bright green bushy moss is not like the flat moss that grows on tree stumps or on the roofs of houses. For one thing, sphagnum can absorb up to ten times its own weight in water. It also sucks the nutrients out of the water, making the water even more acid and nutrient-poor. Few plants can survive in these conditions and any trees, such as the willow or alder, are killed off. Only plants that can tolerate acid conditions can survive. Examples include cranberries and cotton sedges, and carnivorous plants such as sundews, which get extra nutrients by trapping and digesting insects. Areas like this are known as bogs.

What's in a name?

Bogs and fens are very different types of wetlands. Fens may also be called marshes, although this term is more usually used to describe wetland areas near coasts, which are affected by the ocean. In addition, many people include the rivers, pools, and streams that help create the wetlands in the term *wetlands*. In the end, the names given to wetlands are not that important. Gaining a better understanding of them is.

Insect-eating plants

The sundew is a small, harmless-looking bog plant. But its oval, fleshy leaves are death traps for passing insects. The leaves are covered with hundreds of stalked glands—sticky "hairs" that trap the insects that land on them. Once an insect is trapped, the leaf closes over; then the leaf glands release juices that digest the insect. After a few days, all that remain are the insect's wings and hard outer body, which blow away in the wind. The plant has removed much-needed nutrients from the insect's body, since it cannot obtain enough of these from the nutrient-poor soil.

Right This common sundew has trapped an insect. Once the insect has been caught by the plant's sticky hairs, it has no chance of escape.

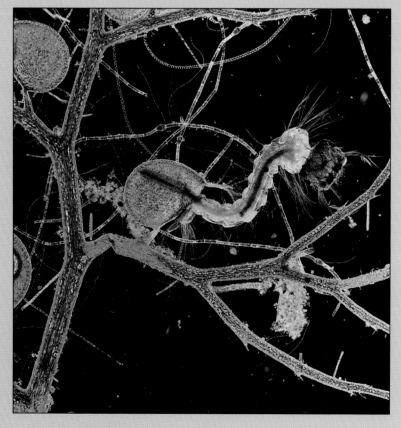

Even more amazing is the bladderwort, which grows in peaty, nutrient-poor water. These floating plants have no roots, but tiny underwater bladders that act like spring-loaded traps. When sensitive hairs at the end of the bladder are touched by a small water creature, such as a water flea, a flap opens inward, sucking in water together with the water flea. The flea is rapidly digested, the nutrients taken up by the plant, and the trap resets, ready for the next victim.

A greater bladderwort. This mosquito larva has triggered the trap and is about to be sucked into the plant's bladder.

3. LIVING BETWEEN THE WATER AND THE LAND

An oystercatcher probes for small shellfish with its powerful bill.

In the early morning, perhaps as the tide creeps in over the silver mudflats of an estuary, life in the wetland begins to stir. A sandworm, gaping jaws ready, moves rapidly over the mud with powerful movements of its body. It encounters an unlucky sand shrimp; there is a brief struggle and the shrimp is still. The sandworm begins to feed. But suddenly a shadow looms over it, a beak stabs down and the worm becomes the first meal of an oystercatcher's day.

Meanwhile, ten inches down in the mud, a bivalve mollusk opens its two shells and extends a long tube upward. The tube, or siphon,

A lugworm next to its wormcast. The spines that point backward help it stay anchored in its burrow.

moves delicately over the surface of the mud like a vacuum cleaner, sucking in water that contains small particles of food and brings life-giving oxygen to the mollusk. The tube touches a marsh snail trundling slowly over the surface, feeding on the tiny algae that cover the mud particles. A shore crab sidles past, claws raised menacingly, and the bivalve hurriedly withdraws its siphon to the safety of the mud below. The snail is not so quick.

This is a typical scene in a temperate salt marsh anywhere in the world. And, as in other types of wetlands, these permanently wet places are not easily invaded by people, so they make a relatively safe refuge for hundreds of different types of birds and other small animals.

Because wetlands are often permanently wet, often underwater, and sometimes influenced by the sea, they provide a special set of conditions that suit certain plants and animals but not others. These plants and animals are adapted to living between the water and the land.

Above Wading birds flock at the edge of the Wadden Zee in the Netherlands searching for food. These birds are dunlins and knots, which are types of sandpipers.

Beaks

One way of understanding how wildlife has adapted to wetlands is to look at one of the most common types of animals found there. Many birds are well adapted to life in the wetlands, in part because they have developed particular beaks or bills suitable for this habitat.

Beaks are birds' knives and forks (and hands to some extent), and different beaks serve different purposes. The type of beak a bird has is a clue as to what kind of food it eats. For example, birds with daggerlike bills, such as bitterns, stab their prey (such as frogs, fish, and even young birds); shoveler ducks move their beaks rapidly over the water surface, sieving out small animals; geese crop grass, the way sheep do.

Some birds have beaks designed to probe the mud for food. They are adapted to particular food; so they have beaks of different lengths (see the diagram below). If all birds had similar bills, they would compete for the same food.

Having a stable food supply is not the only requirement for staying alive. In wetland habitats the right feet are also necessary. Frogs, ducks, and otters all have webbed feet, whereas many water-dwelling insects have fringes of hair, which act as paddles, along their legs.

Bills with a purpose: the different bill lengths enable each bird to prey on different food species. They do not have to compete too much with one another.

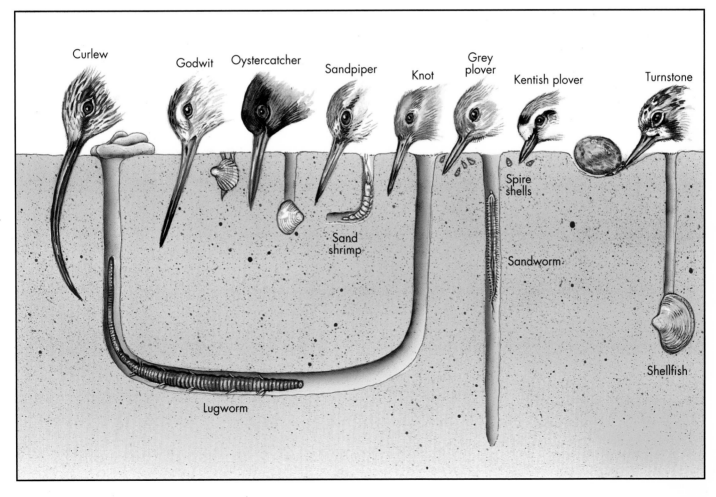

Stick in the muds?

The mudflats of estuaries, seashores, and salt marshes provide an ideal habitat for many burrowing animals. Because these areas are usually tidal, they are alternately covered with water and exposed to the air. By burrowing below the surface when the tide is out, animals are fairly safe from predators such as birds. When the tide returns they may come to the surface or put out siphons or tentacles to pick up food. Others, such as the lugworm, munch their way through the sediment to obtain their meals; giant worm casts that appear when the lower shore is exposed by the outgoing tide are evidence of lugworms.

Above A salt marsh ablaze with sea lavender

Left A salt marsh at low tide. Notice the many different kinds of birds on the mudflats and a sailboat in the distance.

Plant adaptations

Plants also show adaptations to life in wetlands. Chapter 2 describes the creation of a marsh and shows how different plants become more dominant at different stages in the development of fens. On salt marshes, the vegetation will vary, depending on how well it has adapted to the amount of salinity (saltiness) in the marsh. Eelgrass and cordgrass thrive in salt water, but where the mud is exposed at low tide, a cactuslike plant called glasswort may take over. These plants cope with high salinity by expelling salt from their fleshy leaves through special glands.

Higher up the shore more widespread plants that can withstand a limited amount of seawater can be found. Farther away still, plants that can tolerate sea spray but cannot be covered by water are abundant. In summer, the upper regions of salt marshes can be as colorful as any garden on land.

Incredible breathing roots

Mangrove trees grow in mud in which oxygen levels are often low. All living organisms need oxygen to survive, and the black mangrove has adapted to these low-oxygen conditions by producing aerial roots, called pneumatophores. These grow above the mud surface and allow the tree to take in oxygen. Another species, the red mangrove, has fantastically shaped roots called prop roots. These grow out of the mud and support the tree when the tide is out. The roots of mangrove trees are important because they bind the mud together and prevent land from eroding (washing away).

A mangrove tree in a Kenyan swamp. Roots growing from the stem support the tree when the water level is low.

Life in mangrove swamps

An enormous variety of wildlife is found in mangrove swamps. Crabs live in the mud and scuttle around the jungle of roots. Whelks crawl on the roots, and birds nest in the branches of the mangrove trees. When the roots are covered with water, many fish shelter among them, and one fish, the mudskipper, behaves very strangely. Using its specially shaped fins, it will climb out of the water and up the mangrove roots.

Two mudskippers in a dispute over territory. The angle at which they face each other usually decides which fish is going to win.

Below A food web in a salt marsh habitat. The seaweed and algae depend on the sun for their energy. When the organisms shown here die, they will be recycled as nutrients in decaying matter.

Everyone needs neighbors

Living things do not exist in isolation. They live in communities, each depending on others for survival in some way. Some of the members of the community, such as snails, shrimp, and microscopic bacteria, might be thought of as scavengers, feeding on dead animals and plants and recycling them to provide nutrients for other organisms.

Predators might be thought of as population controllers, helping to limit the numbers of other animals. Others act as transporters, carrying seeds, pollen, or even other animals and plants to new locations where they can then colonize.

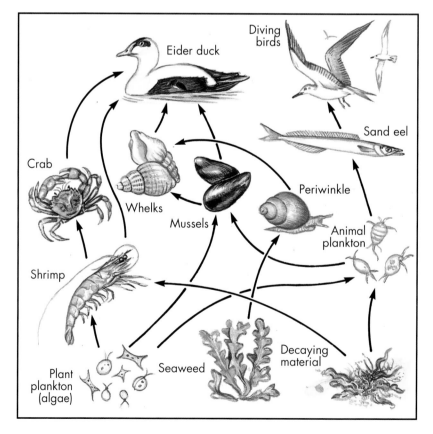

Eider duck — Diving birds — Sand eel — Crab — Whelks — Mussels — Periwinkle — Animal plankton — Shrimp — Decaying material — Plant plankton (algae) — Seaweed

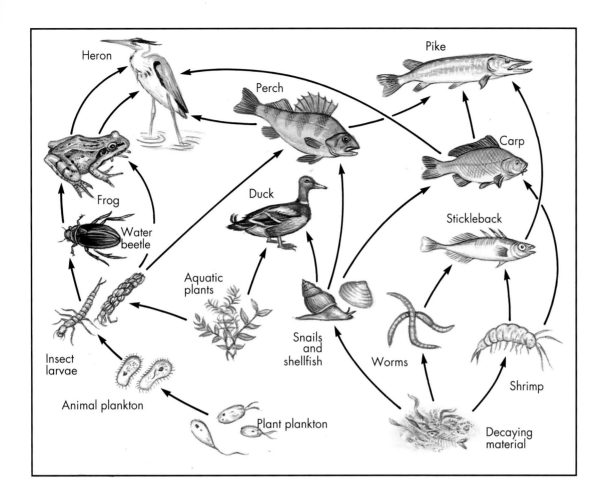

A typical food web in a freshwater wetland habitat. Notice that some of the larger animals at the top of the web have no natural predators, apart from humans.

Each of the animals and plants in the community has a particular role or job— even if that job is to be eaten by something else! They are all part of a food web.

Back to the sun

What supports these communities and enables them to exist? The food webs demonstrate that all animals are ultimately dependent on plants; and plants depend on the energy of the sun and decayed matter to grow and reproduce. Their leaves trap sunlight and use the energy to convert a gas called carbon dioxide from the air and water and to convert nutrients from the soil into food (carbohydrates). This process is called photosynthesis. The sun is therefore the source of all life.

Breaking the web

This interdependence is the reason that communities and the habitats that support them are important. What might happen to the web if one of the strands were to break? What would happen if many strands were removed? The whole community may be damaged when parts of it are damaged. When humans destroy habitats, or even parts of them, whole communities, not just a few types of animals or plants, are at risk. That is one reason why it is so important to preserve our wetlands.

4. PEOPLE AND WETLANDS

For thousands of years, humans have depended on wetlands for their survival. Most of the great ancient civilizations, such as those of Egypt, India, and Mesopotamia (now Iran and Iraq), depended on the fertile wetlands around their great rivers (the Nile, Ganges, and Euphrates, respectively) for their food. When these areas were exhausted through overcultivation, many of these great empires fell.

Above The low-lying land around the Nile River in Egypt is flooded regularly, making the soil nutrient rich and well-suited to agriculture.

Food for all

Even without human involvement, wetlands are one of the most productive natural sources of food in the world. Coastal wetlands are often called "aquatic farmlands" because of their importance as spawning grounds for fish, including shellfish such as lobsters and shrimp. Two-thirds of the commercial fish caught in the United States spawn in wetlands. Practically all the herring caught in the North Sea hatched in the shallow seas and marshlands of the Wadden Sea in the Netherlands. Salt marshes and estuaries are also a source of edible shellfish such as cockles.

Inland wetlands connected to lakes and rivers also provide food and income for millions of people. More than 25,000 villagers living around Lake Chilwa on the Malawi-Mozambique border in East Africa get most of their protein and income from the rich fisheries around the edges of the lake.

The inner Niger Delta in the Saharan country of Mali floods every year, spilling its nutrient-rich waters across 8,000 square miles of the driest land in the country. More than 2.5 million cattle, sheep, and goats graze the delta's

Right Cockle gatherers on the Gower, a peninsula in South Wales. The cockles are sieved out of the sand, collected in buckets, and loaded onto the waiting tractor.

Left Large amounts of fish are herded into traps off the coast of Ceará State in northeast Brazil.

From Lake Titicaca in Peru, reeds and fish provide for many of the needs of the local people and their livestock.

rich vegetation for six months of the year. Plains found in the lower reaches of rivers in temperate lands also form naturally fertile agricultural land because regular winter flooding leaves behind rich sediment.

At Lake Titicaca, more than 12,000 feet up in the Andes Mountains in South America, local people harvest submerged aquatic plants called *yacco*, which are fed to herds of cattle and vicuña (animals like llamas). Reeds are harvested for building, and 6,500 tons of fish are caught and eaten every year.

Food from the wild

The rice plant has been bred from a species of wetland grass and now forms the staple food source of over half the world's population. It is grown in over a hundred countries, but it is particularly well suited to the hot, wet countries of Southeast Asia.

Rice is cultivated in fields called paddies, which have banks of mud built up around the edges. In hilly areas, such as the Philippines, the hillsides are leveled into a series of terraces.

Oil palm, originally from the wetlands of West Africa, is now an excellent source of edible vegetable oil worldwide. Sago palm, native to the swamps of Southeast Asia, is a source of sago flour, the staple food of the Papuans in New Guinea and the Amerindians of the Amazon River Basin.

Young rice plants are transplanted into flooded paddies.

24

The drainage basin of the Amazon forms a gigantic patchwork of wetlands, where the plants and animals support hundreds of thousands of local people in forest communities.

Draining the wetlands

Since wetlands are often very fertile areas, it is hardly surprising that humans should wish to cultivate them. Unfortunately, the main cereal crops of temperate areas, such as wheat and barley, will not withstand flooding or inadequate drainage. The history of much of our temperate wetlands, therefore, has been one of artificial drainage; that is, removing water from the land to make it more suitable for cereal crops.

People have been draining wetlands for a long time. Much of the Netherlands has been built up by the reclamation of salt- and freshwater marshes from about A.D. 1000 to this day. Centuries earlier, the Romans built a network of canals, draining 175,000 acres of an area of Italy known as the Pontine Marshes. They also drained much of Great Britain's wetlands, particularly an area known as the Fens, in East Anglia. The Romans were great engineers: they built canals and diverted major rivers to improve drainage. The Car Dyke is the biggest artificial watercourse ever built in the Fens and runs along its western edge for 90 miles between the towns of Lincoln and Cambridge.

Drainage canals in a national park in Germany. The land in the foreground has been drained to allow sheep to graze.

Windmills have been used for pumping water for hundreds of years.

Drainage systems

Most large-scale drainage systems consist of surface drains—ditches lined with clay or another nonporous substance—and smaller tile pipes laid below the soil surface. The surface drains allow rain or floodwater to be removed quickly; the underground pipes remove groundwater and lower the water table (the level below which the ground is saturated with water). Both surface and below-ground drains are designed to move water away from the drained area by gravity. Sometimes, however, pumps are used. In the 1700s, pumps were powered by windmills, but these were replaced in the nineteenth century by steam pumps. Now the pumps are driven by diesel fuel or electricity.

Wetlands are not drained solely for agriculture. Sometimes they are drained for mining, road construction, or building. In tropical and subtropical areas where waterborne diseases such as malaria are common, the land may also be drained to control the mosquitoes, which carry the disease, that live by the water.

Peat and heat

In many wetlands the normal processes of decay do not occur and the tough, fibrous parts of dead plant material remain as humus or peat instead of returning as nutrients to the earth. Over hundreds or thousands of years, this peat builds up to form a layer several feet thick.

Once it had been discovered that peat could be burned as a fuel, its extraction became a major industry. The whole of the Norfolk Broads, a series of large, shallow lakes in the region of East Anglia in England, are now known to have been created by peat digging, which was carried out on a massive scale in the twelfth and thirteenth centuries. Even until quite recently, peat was dug by hand, using long-handled, thin-bladed spades. Now it is a highly mechanized business.

In certain parts of the world—for example, the former Soviet Union, Ireland, and Germany—peat is still an important fuel used both for domestic heating and for electricity production. In Ireland and Scotland, peat is used in manufacturing whiskey, giving the liquor a distinctive, smoky flavor.

In the 1980s, on the Scottish island of Islay, conservationists campaigned against the decision of a whiskey-making company to dig peat from an important wetland site for migrating Greenland white-fronted geese. However, the local people supported the company because they believed their jobs might be lost if the company could not dig the peat. Finally, in 1987, after testing other wetland sites, the company agreed to take its peat from elsewhere. In 1989 the Islay site, Duich Moss, was protected by European law as a Special Protection Area.

However, the main use for peat today is as a fertilizer. It is sold in large bags in garden centers, hardware stores, and supermarkets to satisfy the seemingly endless demand from gardeners.

Peat cutting in County Galway in Ireland. The peat blocks are turned and stacked to allow them to dry before being collected.

Wetlands out of concrete

As rivers and lakes grow and change, vast deposits of sand and gravel—resources needed for the construction of roads and buildings—are laid down.

All over the world, the extraction of these valuable materials has become a major industry in recent years and, as a result, has caused much local damage to habitats in the form of huge pits. However, many of these pits have been flooded and have turned back into valuable wetland habitats.

Experiments have shown that the best habitats are obtained when these new lakes have irregular edges with bays and promontories, shallow margins to encourage wetland plants, and offshore islands to provide secure nesting sites.

The disappearing thatcher

For much of human history, reed beds have been cut for thatching, which makes long-lasting, waterproof roofing. Thatchers were once common in village communities, but now few reed beds are cultivated commercially. A few marsh men are still employed in the Norfolk Broads, cutting the reed beds every two years and tying the reeds into bundles for drying. Cutting the reeds and managing the water level in the reed beds with sluice gates has helped preserve these habitats for hundreds, perhaps thousands, of years. Without special management, they gradually change and become invaded by scrub, alder, and willow, as these plants begin their slow succession to dry land.

Harvesting reeds in marshlands in Overijssel in the Netherlands. Most reed-cutting is still done by hand. The reeds are gathered into bundles and allowed to dry.

The complete wetland

A single wetland, such as a mangrove swamp, will produce wood for fuel, for building, and for paper manufacture. The bark is also a valuable source of tannin, which is used by the leather industry, and the leaves make a rich fodder for domestic animals. The waters are rich in fish, crustaceans (shrimp and crabs), and shellfish (oysters, mussels, and clams). Wild animals and beekeeping provide a source of meat and honey.

Wetlands are important as habitats in their own right, and they are important to the economy of human communities.

29

5. CELEBRATING WETLANDS

Wetlands not only sustain us in practical ways, they also are a source of inspiration for some of the best literature. Wetlands are often wild and beautiful places that stir the imagination. The description of a marsh by Charles Dickens on page 4 is one example. It is interesting to see how wetlands are depicted—often as threatening, lonely, wild, sinister, silent, or dangerous.

Some poetry has also been inspired by wetlands. An unknown Egyptian composed this poem over two thousand years ago:

The reed-cutter travels to the Delta to get arrows;
When he has done more than his arms can do,
Mosquitoes have slain him,
Gnats have slaughtered him,
He is quite worn out!

Above A wetland hunting party in the middle of the nineteenth century. Hunting wild fowl is still popular today, but it is carefully controlled so that wild bird populations are not threatened. Many people feel that killing wild animals for sport is no longer justifiable.

Here is a short piece from *The Song of Hiawatha* by American poet Henry Wadsworth Longfellow:

And the bull-frog, the Dahinda,
Thrust his head into the moonlight,
Fixed his yellow eyes upon him,
Sobbed and sank beneath the surface;
And anon a thousand whistles,

Answered over all the fenlands,
And the heron, the Shuh-shuh-gah,
Far off in the reedy margin,
Heralded the hero's coming,
Westward thus fared Hiawatha.

These are some of the many examples of wetlands in literature.

A picture of water-lilies by French painter Claude Monet. Notice how well the artist portrays the reflections in the water.

6. THE DESTRUCTION OF WETLANDS

Above Pollution from industry can harm the delicate ecology of wetland areas.

Despite their importance, wetlands have often been seen as wastelands – breeding grounds for mosquitoes, disease-ridden, and fit only to be drained, "improved," or filled in. An estimated 50 percent of all wetlands in the United States have been drained for agriculture and other purposes. Iowa had plowed over 99 percent of its natural marshes by the beginning of the 1980s. In Great Britain, the Fens are less than 1 percent of the size they were when records were first made in the seventeenth century. Up to two-thirds of Europe's wetlands have already disappeared.

Sinking and shrinking
One effect of draining and cultivation is that the land shrinks as it dries out, so the surface sinks. In some areas, such as the Fens, where large amounts of peat have also been removed, houses, bridges, and railroads have subsided (sunk) and now lean at strange angles. Some rivers are now perched thirteen feet above the surrounding farmland!

Spring flowers in a temperate meadow. Scenes such as this are becoming increasingly rare as meadows are drained for growing cereals or to make dry pastureland.

Disappearing habitats

The draining of wetlands, peat extraction, and increased cultivation alter the habitats in a way that make them no longer capable of supporting their original wildlife communities. In temperate regions, such as in parts of the United States and northern Europe, a number of insect species that live in slow-flowing water have become extinct. Other species have become rare, such as the bittern, otter, and even the so-called common frog.

Plant species have also suffered. In the past, low-lying fields that flooded regularly (water meadows) were used for grazing cattle. The floodwater

A helicopter sprays insecticide on a lake in the Camargue in France. The insecticide will disrupt the ecology of the wetland.

warmed the land in winter, allowing the early growth of grass. In July the meadows would be cut for a late hay crop, allowing wildflowers to bloom and produce seeds. The flowers attracted butterflies and other insects which, in turn, attracted birds, small reptiles, and mammals. Now, most of the water meadows have been drained and planted with grass species that exclude other plants—and the wildlife communities have gone.

Similar changes have occurred throughout the world. In the Florida Everglades, drainage, flood control, and extraction (removal) of water for urban use have reduced the level of Lake Okeechobee, which feeds the swamps. The flooded area is smaller each year, and this reduces the food available to wading birds and other animals. In the last 60 years, the number of birds in the Everglades has been reduced by as much as 90 percent, from 1,500,000 to less than 150,000.

The manatee, a large, slow-moving aquatic mammal also found in subtropical wetlands such as the Everglades, is threatened with extinction. Habitat destruction and injury from the propellers of motorboats are the main causes.

A Caribbean manatee, or sea cow. Its nose was scarred by a boat propeller.

Blaming the caiman
The caiman is a species of crocodile living in South America. It feeds on fish and was killed by local fishermen who saw it as a competitor. Killing the caimans, however, did not increase the number of fish—in fact, numbers fell. Waste materials produced by the caiman enriched the water, supporting microscopic plants (algae). These plants were at the base of the food web that supported the fish. There was room for fishermen only when there was room for the caiman.

Preparing pesticides for spraying on the crops on a farm in south Florida.

The creeping menace

Just as deadly as the direct destruction of habitats are the effects of pollutants on wetlands. Many pollutants are the result of agriculture. Modern farming methods have provided a way for poisonous waste from farm animals to get into water courses, killing fish and other organisms. Cut grass stored over the winter as silage can also cause leakage of nutrients into rivers and streams. The water becomes super-rich and algae multiply, removing oxygen from the water.

Fertilizers running off the land into this small pond have caused it to become so rich in nutrients that algae grow out of control, blocking out sunlight.

Beside the sea

Estuaries are rich in wildlife, but they are often ideal for human development. Docks and ports, power plants, factories, towns, marinas, and sports complexes are all necessary for economic growth. Seven of the world's ten largest cities, including New York and London, are built on what were once wetland sites. Such development usually destroys wetland habitats. Finding a harmonious balance between development and habitat conservation is not easy.

The death of the Aral Sea. These fishing boats are now stranded many miles from any water and will never fish here again.

The Aral Sea disaster

The Aral Sea in Kazakhstan was the fourth largest body of inland water in the world. Forty thousand tons of sturgeon, carp, and bream were fished each year. Around the sea was fertile wetland used for growing crops and grazing animals.

In the 1960s, water was diverted from the two main rivers feeding the sea to irrigate cotton crops. The irrigation caused nutrients to be leached from the soil, until farming became dependent on artificial fertilizers as well as on large quantities of herbicides and pesticides. Toxic sprays were also used to remove the leaves of the plants in order to harvest the cotton. The leaves were fed to cattle, poisoning the milk and meat that the local population drank and ate.

Meanwhile, as the water level continued to fall, the water became increasingly salty. Much of the sea finally turned to desert, sending up huge dust clouds containing toxic salts. Now drinking water is contaminated and the soil is too salty to grow crops. The fishing industry is destroyed, and 30 million people are at risk from toxic chemicals. Much of this damage may now be impossible to repair.

Because of their position, estuaries often make ideal industrial sites, and then the wetlands suffer. However, some areas have been protected, such as this site on the Tees estuary in northern England, which is a refuge for wildfowl.

In the delta region of the Mississippi River, oil has been found in large amounts, and more than 22,000 oil wells have been drilled to extract it. To make transportation and oil exploration easier, canals have been dug through the swamps. The canals also allow seawater from the Gulf of Mexico to penetrate the freshwater swamps, harming the balance of plants and animals in the Mississippi delta.

Dam construction

Some developing countries have become involved in building massive dams that generate electricity to aid their development. These projects can bring many benefits. For example, the Aswân Dam on the Nile has allowed Egypt to bring electricity to almost all of its villages; and as a result of a dam built on the São Francisco River in northeast Brazil an estimated one million jobs were created.

However, such projects can also do great damage to the wetlands and the animal and plant communities that live there. For example, on the Nile, where the Aswân Dam controls flooding, the silt from floodwater no longer enriches the soil; as a result, costly, less effective artificial fertilizers have to be used instead. The loss of regular flooding also means that the culture of local people, which is based around the river's cycle of flooding, will be changed or lost.

Fish stocks can be destroyed because the dams prevent the fish from reaching their breeding grounds. For example, the rich Columbia River salmon fisheries in North America declined dramatically after dams were built there. Many of the wetland sites destroyed by dams, particularly those in Africa, are important sites for migrating birds that spend the winter there.

Still losing ground?

The Pantanal in Brazil is the largest wetland in the world. It provides a habitat for the giant otter, maned wolf, marsh deer, and yacare caiman. Hundreds of thousands of caiman are poached every year. Hyacinth macaws (a parrotlike bird) are sold for $8,000 a pair in the United States and $12,000 in Europe. As a result of the trade in these magnificent birds, less than 3,000 macaws remain in the wild.

The removal of forests around the edges of the Pantanal and the burning of grasslands to make way for cattle ranching threaten the balance of the wetland. Drainage for agriculture, pollution due to erosion, and toxic waste from sugarcane processing and gold mining are damaging the ecology of the area.

There are a few encouraging signs, however. Some landowners understand the need to protect the area; others realize that commercial caiman farming would protect wild populations and bring in more income. But the destruction continues. Part of the land is protected as the Pantanal National Park—but that part is less than 2 percent of the Pantanal wetland. The next chapter looks at how the needs of people can be balanced against the need to protect our wetland habitats.

Above The world's largest dam site at Itaipu in Brazil. Even though there are benefits from dams such as this, they have to be balanced against the damage they cause to the ecology of the region.

7. WETLANDS FOR THE FUTURE

There is a close relationship between people and wetlands. But unless we can develop our relationship with wetlands in less damaging ways, we risk destroying them forever.

Does it really matter if wetlands or other habitats are destroyed? Some of the ways in which people benefit from wetlands are described in earlier chapters, but there are many others. For example, wetlands help control flooding by soaking up water during heavy rainfall and then releasing it slowly. A six-inch rise in a ten acre marsh puts more than 1.5 million gallons of water in storage. Mangrove swamps protect the land from soil erosion and the effects of storms.

Wetlands also act as a form of pollution control, naturally filtering out industrial and human waste. Reeds need oxygen around their roots. To obtain it the plants absorb oxygen through their leaves and pump it down their stems into the mud below. The oxygen allows microorganisms in the mud to break down polluting substances, similar to the way that some sewage treatment plants operate. Several towns in Germany now treat their town sewage using natural methods. A salt lake outside Calcutta has acted as a natural sewage treatment plant for over 50 years. The Alcovy River Swamp in Georgia saves taxpayers an estimated $10 million every year in controlling pollution.

Farming alligators in a Louisiana wetland. The young alligators are raised and then released into the wild, where they will later be hunted for their skins and meat.

Perhaps even more importantly, wetlands act as a reservoir for greenhouse gases, absorbing millions of tons of carbon dioxide every year during photosynthesis and trapping it for thousands of years within the peat. It is likely, therefore, that wetlands are also important in the regulation of climate.

Even if wetlands were not important for all these reasons, they are worth preserving for their own sake. Wetlands are places of great beauty, supporting perhaps a tenth of all the world's species; they were in existence for millions of years before humans evolved on this planet. Can we really allow ourselves to contribute to wetland destruction?

Sustainable wetlands

We have to learn to use wetlands in such a way that we do not damage them, either now or in the future. This is the principle of sustainable development. A definition was put forward by the Commission on Environment and Development in 1987. It said, "Sustainable development means meeting the needs of the present without compromising the ability of future generations to meet their own needs." An expanded definition might say something about *why* we should manage the earth's resources wisely.

In June 1992, all the world's major countries met in Rio de Janeiro at a United Nations conference called the Earth Summit. One of the results was a set of principles known as the Rio Declaration. The first principle states: "Human beings are at the center of concerns for sustainable development. They are entitled to a healthy and productive life in harmony with nature."

Nearly all the countries in the world signed this declaration. The second sentence would be hard to argue with. But the first sentence must be understood as a long-term goal. Concerns that may seem beneficial to humans in the short term may actually harm us, as well as other species, over time.

An airboat skims the surface of the Everglades in Florida. Tourists can bring much-needed income to help protect wetlands in their natural state.

Agreeing to protect the wetlands

One way of protecting wetlands is through national laws and international agreements. As long ago as 1971, the Convention on Wetlands of International Importance agreed on measures to protect important wetland sites. This agreement, called the Ramsar Convention, after the city in Iran where the conference took place, has now been signed by over sixty countries.

A herd of lechwe (antelope) move in safety in the Okavango Delta in Botswana.

More than 530 sites worldwide are now designated Ramsar sites, although this does not give them automatic protection. They include the Coongie Lakes and Kakadu National Park in Australia, the Volga Delta in Russia and Kazakhstan, the Bangweulu Swamps in Zambia, the Camargue in France, Lough Neagh in Northern Ireland, the Everglades and Chesapeake Bay in the United States, Polar Bear Provincial Park in Canada, and the Machalilla in Equador. The threatened Pantanal in Brazil and the Okavango Delta in Botswana, however, are not Ramsar sites.

Most countries also have their own forms of national or local protection, such as national parks and nature reserves. Such protection is not total, however. The need for more development, such as road building or the extraction of minerals, can still place them in danger.

The Earth Summit in 1992 produced a plan called Agenda 21, which was designed to safeguard the world's resources. Two of the longest chapters are about the protection of seas and coastal areas and the protection of fresh water and freshwater habitats. But although Agenda 21 is very important, it is not legally binding. This means that countries will try to keep to the agreements and principles Agenda 21 sets out, but much will depend on whether they have enough money to enforce them. Success will also depend on countries cooperating with each other, and richer countries may have to be prepared to make some changes and sacrifices.

Even when wetlands themselves are protected, they can be damaged by the drainage of nearby land or by pollution from elsewhere. Other ways of protecting wetlands must be found.

Gardening needs

If we are to protect the environment, we have to change the way we do things. For example, many people now no longer buy gardening supplies that use peat. Alternatives have been developed, such as compost made from coconut husks or straw; demand for peat has therefore been greatly reduced. This may be the single most important factor in saving what remains of Earth's peat bogs. This does not necessarily mean that peat should never be used. In undisturbed wetlands, peat will build up at a rate of about 1.3 tons per acre per year. Some of it could still be used if this is less than the rate at which it forms. This is another example of the principle of sustainability. Many people would argue, however, that all use should be stopped to allow our damaged wetlands to recover.

Cut peat is loaded for transportation from a Swedish site. Extracting the peat damages the surface vegetation and changes the conditions of the soil, irreversibly altering the habitat.

Could the way we do things be changed or improved so that wetland damage is reduced? For example, with better pollution control, less intensive farming, and building smaller-scale dams, the future of wetlands would be brighter. Although this may cause some inconvenience, many of these changes would be beneficial in ways other than safeguarding wetlands. Nobody wants polluted water, and many people are now demanding meat or cereals that are produced in more organic ways.

Turning back the tide

As well as the possibility of changing the way we do things to preserve wetlands, people are now finding that it makes sense to create wetlands. The Bangladeshi government encourages the planting of mangroves along its coast to assist with flood defense. A European Community–funded project in Wales involves the planting of reed beds to combat contamination of the Pelenna River from old mine workings. A wetland plant, the water hyacinth, is cultivated to produce a natural fertilizer in the Sudan and processed to make methane gas for homes in the United States.

But wetlands can only really be safe if we change the way we think about them. Once we understand that they are naturally rich environments that give their best when we work in harmony with them, we can go a long way to protecting them forever.

8. SO WHAT CAN I DO?

Changing people's buying habits can be a very effective way of bringing about environmental change. Individuals can influence what happens to the environment if enough of them act together. This final chapter gives some examples of what individuals can do in the vital task of saving the world's wetlands.

Change how you live

Changing how you live, or changing your lifestyle, can be beneficial whether you take small steps or drastic steps. Educating others about the importance of natural habitats is a start. Buying organically grown vegetables, flour, or meat reduces the use of chemical fertilizers, pesticides, and animal feeds.

The food will cost a little more, but only by increasing the number of people who want these products will more stores stock them, more farmers be willing to grow them, and more prices be reduced.

Avoid polluting water by using environment-friendly cleaning products. And be careful what you wash down the drain. Take household oil and chemicals, including old batteries, to a local collection site, where they will be disposed of properly. Use less water. This could mean using low-water toilets or taking a quick shower instead of a bath.

The soil in this flower bed has been nourished by adding compost made from coconut fiber rather than peat moss.

Taking practical action

Join a young people's organization that carries out local environmental projects. The organization will be involved with other habitats as well as wetlands, but it is important to remember that all environments are connected in some way—nothing lives in isolation. The library or chamber of commerce will have details of environmental organizations; a few are listed on page 47. Some schools even offer school credit for environmental projects like cleaning up wetlands.

You can go one step further and create your own wetland. This could be a small pond on your school or club grounds. These are more effective (and will attract more wildlife) if you create marshy areas around the pond. This can be tricky, and you'll have to obtain permission, but there will be local organizations or individuals who can advise you. Your project need not be expensive. It is often possible to borrow equipment such as spades and shovels and materials such as pond liner might be donated—and the labor should not cost anything (you and your friends!). One important thing to think about is how you can be sure that your mini-wetland will still be around in a couple of years. Think about long-term maintenance (if necessary, seek advice). This might suggest another meaning for the word sustainable.

You could also become a wetland detective and stop any unnecessary pollution. Look for any signs of pollution—for example, strange smelling or colored water, foam, and dead fish, or even for trucks dumping anything suspicious in or near streams, rivers, or canals. Contact your local department of the environment if you notice these things.

Above Garbage dumped in rivers and ended up stranded by the tide in this estuary. Some of it just looks ugly, but some may damage the fragile wetland environment.

Speaking out

Many people working together can have a very great effect on protecting the environment. It is important that people know about and understand issues such as the importance of wetlands. There may be opportunities to produce a display about wetlands in your school or club or even in the local shopping mall. People are often unaware of what is on their own doorstep. You may find out about plans that could threaten a local pond or damage a piece of wetland, and you might want to do something to protect it.

You could support a local organization that protests or lobbies to stop development. But remember there are always at least two sides to any argument. Development is not in itself a bad thing—without it we would not have many of the good things that we enjoy. But development has to be appropriate; that is, it needs to take into account the needs of people and the needs of the environment. We need to seek balance in all things. We need sustainable wetlands.

It is possible to have sustainable wetlands. Here you can see people and wildlife in harmony in the Okefenokee swamps in Georgia.

GLOSSARY

Adapted Changed to suit or fit different conditions.

Algae Simple plants that grow in water or moist ground.

Bacteria Kinds of microorganisms found in the air, water, earth, and in bodies. Some bacteria are beneficial; some cause disease.

Bivalve mollusk One of a group of animals with hard shells, made up of two hinged halves, and gills for breathing.

Bog Wet, spongy ground, often surrounded by water, rich in plant matter.

Colonize To become established in a new environment.

Decomposing Rotting away.

Diverted Turned aside or deflected.

Ecology The relationship among living things and their environment.

Endanger To put in danger or at risk

Estuary A body of water composed of freshwater from rivers and saltwater from an ocean.

Evaporate To change into water vapor or steam.

Evolving Developing or changing gradually over a long period.

Extinct When a species dies out completely.

Fen Low land covered partly or wholly with water, unless artificially drained.

Fertility The ability of land to produce crops.

Greenhouse gases Gases in the atmosphere, such as carbon dioxide and methane, believed to trap the sun's heat and cause the warming of the earth's surface.

Habitats The natural homes of animals or plants.

Herbicides Chemicals that destroy plants. They are used to control weeds.

Irrigate To supply land with water, usually to water crops.

Livestock Farm animals.

Marsh A tract of soft wet land usually characterized by grasses and similar plants.

Mechanized Equipped with machinery.

Microscopic Not large enough to be seen with the naked eye, but visible under a microscope.

Migratory Passing regularly from one region to another.

Mudflats A level tract of land lying a little below the surface of water, or alternately covered and left bare by the tide.

Nonporous Not allowing fluid to pass through.

Nutrient A substance essential for growth.

Organisms Living plants and animals.

Pesticides Chemicals used for killing pests, especially insects.

Poached Fish caught or game hunted illegally.

Pollutants Substances that harm or poison the environment.

Predator A bird or animal that attacks and kills other birds or animals for food.

Promontories Fingers of land jutting out into a body of water.

Protein Any of a large number of substances necessary as part of the food for human beings, other animals, and plants.

Reservoir A lake made by humans where water is kept in store.

Safeguard To protect. Anything that gives protection or security.

Salt marsh Flat land subject to overflow by salt water.

Sediment The fine material in lakes and rivers that settles gradually to the bottom.

Silage Semirotted cut grass used as winter animal feed.

Spawning The depositing of eggs by fish.

Species A group of plants or creatures with similar features.

Subtropical A region with a warm climate.

Swamp A wetland often partially covered by water, especially one dominated by trees.

Temperate A region with a moderate climate.

Thatcher A person skilled in making roofs from reeds.

Tropical The hot region around the equator, between two imaginary circles known as the Tropic of Cancer and the Tropic of Capricorn which run around the earth.

Further Reading

Arvetis, Chris and Palmer, Carole. *Swamps and Marshes.* Skokie, IL: Rand McNally, 1994.

Coote, Roger, ed. *Atlas of the Environment.* Milwaukee: Raintree Steck-Vaughn, 1992.

Dixon, Dougal. *The Changing Earth.* Young Geographer. New York: Thomson Learning, 1993.

Fleisher, Paul. *Ecology A to Z.* New York: Dillon Press, 1994.

Javna, John. Fifty Simple Things Kids Can Do to Save the Earth. Kansas City,. MO: Andrews & McMeel, 1990.

Langley, Andrew. *Wetlands.* New York: Reader's Digest Association, 1993.

Place, Robin. *Bodies from the Past.* Digging up the Past. New York: Thomson Learning, 1995.

Rom, Christine Sotnak. *The Everglades.* National Parks. New York: Crestwood House, 1988.

Tesar, Jenny. *Endangered Habitats.* Our Fragile Planet. New York: Facts on File, 1992.

Further Information

For further information about wetlands that are under threat, contact the following environmental organizations:

Center for Environmental Education, Center for Marine Conservation, 1725 De Sales Street NW, Suite 500, Washington, DC 20036

Chesapeake Bay NERR–MD, Maryland Department of Natural Resources, Tawes Office Building, 580 Taylor Avenue, Annapolis, MD 21401

Fish and Wildlife Service, Department of the Interior, Washington, DC 20420

Friends of the Earth (U.S.A.), 218 D Street SE, Washington, DC 20003

Greenpeace U.S.A., 1436 U Street NW, Washington, DC 20009

National Audubon Society, National Education Office, R.R. #1, Box 171, Sharon, CT 06069

National Oceanic and Atmospheric Administration, Department of Commerce, Washington, DC 20230

World Wildlife Fund, 1250 24th Street NW, Washington, DC 20037

Picture acknowledgments
Bruce Coleman/Jan Van De Kam 11, /Hans Reinhard 13, /Jane Burton 14(top), /Kim Taylor 14(bottom), /Jan De Van Kam 15(top), /Dr. Frieder Sauer 15(bottom), /Jan De Van Kam 16, 18(top), /Robert Glover 18(bottom), /Luiz Claudio Margio 23(bottom), /Hans Reinhard 25, /John Murray 27, /Jan De Van Kam 29, /Christer Fredriksson 33, /Jan Canculosi 35(top), /Patrick Clement 35(bottom), /Nicholas De Vore 38, /Dr. Eckart Pott 42, /Bob Glover 43, /Andrew Davies 44. ffotograff/Jill Ranford 8, /Patrick Aithie 23(top). Robert Harding/Christina Gascoigne 12. The Hutchison Library/V. Ivleva 36. Natural History Photographic Agency/John Shaw 7(top), /Darek Karp 9(top), /David Woodfall 19, /Dr. Ivan Polunin 20(top), /David Woodfall 28(bottom), /E. A. Jones *contents,* 33(top), /Norbert Wu 34, /David Woodfall 37, /Anthony Bannister 41. Tony Stone *cover,* /Randy Wells *title page,* /David Maisel 5(top), /Larry Ulrich 5(bottom), /Penny Tweedie 6, /Eric Hayman 7(left), /J. F. Preedy 9(bottom), /A. C. Tidswell 22, /Warren Jacobs 24(top), /Colin Raw 28(top), /Joe Cornish 32, /Keith Wood 39, /Doug Armand 40, /Randy Wells 45. Visual Arts Library 30, 31. Wayland Picture Library 24(bottom), 26. Maps and diagrams on pages 4, 10, 17, 20, 21 by Peter Bull.

INDEX

Numbers in **bold** refer to photographs